I0060349

LEADERSHIP SUPERHEROES AND CORPORATE VILLAINS

TRUE STORIES OF COURAGE AND
COWARDICE IN BUSINESS AND THE LESSONS
WE CAN LEARN FROM THEM

BRUCE WOLF

WOLF MOUNTAIN
– PUBLISHING –

Copyright © 2020 by Wolf Mountain Publishing, LLC

All rights reserved.

No part of this book may be reproduced in any form or by any electronic or mechanical means, including information storage and retrieval systems, without written permission from the author, except for the use of brief quotations in a book review.

ISBN 978-1-952286-09-4 (paperback)

ISBN 978-1-952286-08-7 (ebook)

Dedicated to the superheroes (and villains) who have taught me so much.

CONTENTS

FOREWORD

Have you ever been inspired by a leader? Ever been so motivated by your manager that you strove to do better?

Lots of us have.

Have you ever felt demotivated by a leader? Ever felt so wronged that the only logical explanation was that your manager was just a serial dickhead?

All of us have.

Whether a leader is great or terrible, there's a lot of things we can learn.

But we usually don't.

When we have a great manager, we don't always tell people about it (after all, we don't want to come off as a suck-up). When we have a terrible manager, we usually tell people about it to vent more than to learn and we tend to paint the other person as a mustache-twirling villain who thrives on making people miserable.

Either way, we don't get much out of the discussion, even though there's so much to learn in both cases.

If we can be honest with ourselves about our stories and our emotions, we can learn a lot. If we can share those stories after stripping out the emotion, we can help others learn a lot, too.

Over the years, working at more than a dozen companies, I've been blessed to have some truly great managers, inspirations, dare I say: superheroes.

There's a lot to learn from these people. No one is perfect, the human condition is a flawed one, but damn it, these people were better than most. I consider myself lucky to have worked for them and learned from them.

There's a lot of lessons I picked up through osmosis, without even really thinking about them. And when I step back and examine what happened, there's a lot more to learn than I realized.

I hope I can share some of those lessons in this book.

I've also had some managers that were... decidedly un-superhero-like.

I don't want to come off like a little whiner, but these situations... just plain sucked.

There's a lot to learn from them, as well. But it requires going deeper. When we're wronged (especially in the workplace), we have a tendency to just write people off as bad guys. That kind of thinking, the embracing of the natural human emotions which serve as a defense mechanism for our fragile little egos, makes things a lot harder on us. We can't learn if we look at these people as cardboard cutout villains.

They're not villains.

They don't do things to be evil.

They do things for a reason (and no, that reason isn't

to take over Metropolis City Bank and make it a secret bad guy headquarters or build a diabolical laser that can blow up the moon).

We may not agree with how these people approach situations and we may not empathize with them, but if we can understand them, we can learn something and we can look for a better way.

If we learn enough, improve ourselves enough, we might even become superheroes to someone else.

A QUICK NOTE

Every superhero has a secret identity. Every villain has a cover. Most people never know who their true identities are.

In this book, every name has been changed.

You may feel like you know them, even if you don't know me.

That's because these stories play out over and over again, by different people in different companies around the world. Much like superhero stories often follow a formula, workplace conflict can start to feel familiar.

As you read, you will gain far more insight by focusing on the lessons at the end of each chapter than by wondering if you know the people themselves.

Focus on what's important.

There's a lot less to learn from Clark Kent than there is from Superman.

1

RICHARD AND FRIENDS

When I wrote software, I always had a pet project.

Actually, I usually had like half a dozen at a time. I just like fiddling around with code. Sometimes it wouldn't go anywhere beyond satisfying my own curiosity. Sometimes it would result in a small improvement in a system I worked on. Every once in a while, it grew bigger.

In one of the really big ones, a third-party firm wasn't living up to what the business sponsors wanted. They were charging everything they said they would, but the features really weren't there. The worst part was, this was a pretty simple system and the third-party firm just kept trying to make every piece of basic functionality a big expensive upsell.

I saw an opportunity. I had one of those moments where I said, "Psh, I could do this myself! I could do better than all these clowns!"

So I did.

It was a really fun project. I started working on little pieces of it in my spare time and putting together the larger infrastructure as it came together. Every time the third-party firm said they couldn't add a feature to their system, I tried to add it to my version. It actually ended up being easier than I thought.

I talked to my boss about it, and he was supportive. He actually thought it was a good idea and ended up adding a guy named Richard (note: in case you didn't read the front matter, his name wasn't really Richard) from another team to help.

Richard was an old school IT guy. When I say "old school," I don't mean that he started in IT before everything was a phone app, I mean that he started before IT was a thing. He was one of the guys who helped haul in the first desktop computers and those giant bubble screen monitors that weigh more than a refrigerator. Since he knew how to plug in all the cables, he became "one of those IT computer guys" in the early days of IT.

As his career went on, he never really got into coding, but he did pay a lot of attention to how politics worked around the office.

I showed him the code and he kind of nodded and told me it was good stuff. He asked some questions and was generally complimentary of my efforts.

I went back to work, and he called a couple days later to talk about the project, see how it was going, and see if I needed any help.

I told him I was fine, everything was going well, but he did have a couple suggestions. He explained how some business partners might want to use some new features and if I put them in there, it might make it a better product.

I took his feedback and added the features to the program.

He kept in touch as I was working on this program, following up once or twice a week to see the progress, ask questions, and give more suggestions.

I kept working on it, adding features, and making it even better. Along the way, I kept my boss updated on how it was going and he thought it was all good stuff - he just wanted to make sure I was getting more core responsibilities done because this program was still mostly a pet project of mine. Eventually I got it to a usable level, and we partnered to roll things out to some small teams.

Once it started rolling out to some teams, Richard called and said that he had a friend in HR who wanted it. He just wanted me to give him access so he could show it to them.

HR loved it. Richard asked if I could add a couple core features and the system really took off from there.

A couple months later, I was invited to an HR meeting. The invite was really vague and it was with a bunch of people I'd never heard of (I was never partnered with HR).

When I got to the meeting, I quickly realized that this was a surprise recognition meeting!

I was given a nice framed award and a bonus check! It didn't bother me that these were people I'd never met and seemed to have no idea who I was.

What did bother me, though, was that the last award

went to Richard. Well, his award really didn't bother me, it was the things they said about him that bothered me.

They lauded his vision for seeing a need and proactively filling it. They praised him for getting a program that was exactly what they wanted. They clapped after announcing how he was the driving force behind the entire effort.

He smiled and nodded while completely avoiding eye contact with me the entire time.

After the meeting, he totally dodged me. He didn't answer my phone calls. He didn't respond to my emails.

I had to calendar stalk him to find a time he'd be at his desk so I could confront him in person.

When I asked him why the HR executives seemed to think he had the vision for this program and why they seemed to think he was the one filling the need and why they seemed to think he was the driving force behind the effort, he just laughed it off. He sheepishly explained that those were just his friends and that they were exaggerating for him.

I expressed my feelings to my boss, who understood that this entire effort came from my ideas and hard work. He pulled Richard in so we could all talk together. Richard reiterated his story that his friends were just exaggerating for his benefit. My boss stuck up for me and said that it didn't feel that way.

And that was the end of it.

It was also the end of me talking to Richard.

LESSONS

. . .

At the moment, my biggest takeaway here was to never trust anyone.

That's a terrible lesson, though.

Who wants to go through life bitter and distrustful, constantly looking around corners to see who might be waiting in the wings to screw them over?

I don't.

That's a miserable way to go through life.

I felt I needed to look for what I could own, what I could take away from this story in a positive way.

Looking back, I realized that I was putting myself in a bubble. I liked to code and I was basically putting myself in the corner and coding away. I wasn't looking for input, I wasn't getting feedback from other people on what could make the program better (except for Richard's unsolicited input for his friends in HR), and I basically just wasn't being a good business partner.

One of the first things I should have done when I had this idea, was reach out to people from other parts of the organization to see how they might want to use the system. I should have been asking them what would make it more helpful for them and building those ideas into my program.

That's what Richard was doing. He was just doing it secondhand.

I knew these lessons when I started developing the system, though. I just figured it was such a big, gaping need that I could easily fill it without their input. I wanted full control over my pet project without anyone telling me what to do.

Richard showed me that, even when the need is so

great that even a moderately not-terrible solution would be a heavenly gift, outside voices (especially prospective clients) can still offer a lot of valuable insight. Why not make something as useful as possible?

To be honest with you (and with myself), I was enjoying working on this alone. Even though I'm a volume ii extrovert, I still enjoy just pounding through something by myself sometimes. Not being told what to do is a pretty cool thing and I enjoy the control that comes with being the only person with input on how something should run.

That may feel nice in the short-term, but it's really not beneficial in the long-term.

I should have been out involving others, gaining feedback, and making it even better.

I didn't do that, so Richard did.

Once he started doing that, I should have proactively stepped up and cut out the middle man. Instead of playing telephone with the requirements feedback, I should have asked Richard directly to connect me with the clients. "Hey, Richard, I'd like to meet your friends in HR and talk to them about this effort - would you mind introducing me?"

This doesn't have to be out of a distrustful mindset, either - it can be to make connections with people in the spirit of making my software better and more helpful for prospective clients (the fact that it would have also addressed any potentially distrustful paranoia is just a bonus).

Even though I felt wronged and taken advantage of, there are still positive behavioral improvements I can take away from this (which, coincidentally, would also prevent me from feeling wronged and taken advantage of in the future).

But what about Richard?

Is he just an ill-intentioned villain? An evil parasite never to be trusted?

Probably not.

Most people aren't.

If I look back on his story and try to take his word, there are things I can learn there, too.

I'll never know what Richard was thinking. My read on the situation was, is, and always will be tinted by the emotions I felt there.

But if I take his word for it, if I empathize with him and read his story as a guy who was just trying to be helpful and ended up having roses and gratitude unexpectedly heaped on him for no reason, then I can learn and grow.

In that situation, what could he have done differently?

He could have stood up at that awards meeting and said, "You know, what? I appreciate all those kind words, but, really, Bruce is the guy who had the vision from the beginning. He's the guy who really put the hard work in to make sure this filled your needs."

If he had any idea what I might have been feeling, he could have just made a comment to alleviate 80% of any potential ill will.

But turning down a compliment is hard. It goes against human nature. We like being complimented, we strive for compliments - but if he would have turned one down, I wager he would have looked even better to the people who were praising him. Humility is admirable.

He also could have thought ahead and been more proactive.

When he first talked to his friends in HR about the program, he could have included me. He could have been a connector. He could have brought people together for a mutually beneficial relationship that probably would have made the software even better.

In situations like this, people can get fearful of being left behind. Thoughts like "If I introduce these people to each other, they won't need me, I'll be left out of everything" start to creep in.

Fears like that are natural, but what comes next?

Let's say you introduce them and, as your fear of fears would have it, they go on and work without you.

So?

So now they're working fine as partners, appreciative of you for bringing them together. You establish a reputation as a connector, someone who's in the know, a go-to person when you need to meet someone. That reputation grows and more people want to be connected to you.

Then you can spend your time on something more productive and useful than forcing yourself to be a go-between in that relationship.

The alternative is allaying your fears of being left behind by using all your effort to hold on to your position and working to keep people separated so you can be their sole connection to each other. Sure, you won't be left behind, but you'll be using all your energy to cling to a role as a redundant and unnecessary cog to an intentionally inefficient machine.

Is that what you really want?

Leadership Superheroes And Corporate Villains

2

JIMMY AND THE MASTER PLAN

When I was in high school, I never imagined I would start my own business, let alone multiple businesses like I have.

I just figured I would get a job and work at a company like everyone else. I didn't give much thought to how those companies started; they were just big faceless enterprises that gave people jobs so everyone could all make money.

I worked at a few of those places to make money. One of them was a small restaurant chain where I delivered food.

It was a small chain, so I worked directly with the owner, Jimmy, a fair amount. He was a loud, fiery guy and he was absolutely tireless. Every day, he was up at 5:00 am to get the food prep started and he would close the place down at 10:30. Through it all, he was never lacking for energy. I don't know how he did it.

One day, after a couple weeks of working there, Jimmy

gave me an order for delivery and said that after I dropped it off, I should pick up his kid from the public pool and drop him off at home.

What?

Me?

Pick up a kid?

I didn't feel like I should have been trusted with a child.

Heck, I have a bunch of kids now and I still don't think I should be trusted with a child.

And here this guy asked me to pick one up and drop it off like it was a plate of tacos (I shouldn't be trusted around a plate of tacos either, but at least I wasn't going to eat his children.).

So I picked the kid up.

Talk about awkward.

"Hello strange child that I've never met, please get in this strange vehicle that I just learned to drive like a month ago. I'll just take you to a private residence that I've never been to before and hopefully I won't crash into a telephone pole and kill us on the way."

I did it, though (the pickup and drop off part, not the crashing into a telephone pole and killing us both part). It was as awkward as I thought it would be.

It was only slightly less awkward the second time.

A little less the third time.

The guy had a lot of kids and I was running them all over the place between my deliveries.

It felt a little unprofessional. I felt like Jimmy shouldn't have been asking someone who works for him to do personal errands for him.

That was when I realized it: I was working for him. Not for his company, but for *him*.

This meant that I wasn't just punching a clock so someone working at some far-off payment processing facility could cut me a check at the end of the week. No, I was showing up every day face to face with the person who ran the show.

I didn't work for a company, I worked for a person.

Sometimes he would ask me if I could come in early to work with him. Some nights he would ask me if I could come to his house late to drop something off.

It's similar to being asked to work late in other jobs, but not quite the same.

When I got up early to help him, I saw how he acted before the coffee had kicked in. When I went to his house late, I could see the weariness in his shoulders as he sipped his bedtime wine.

I came to realize that, despite what I had previously thought, he wasn't tireless.

He was tired.

But he kept showing up. Every day. At 5:00 am.

When we worked together, he started to tell me more about the business and more about his story.

Both were interesting, but the latter was more interesting.

Jimmy told me about what he was like in high school (none of what he said surprised me at all). "Brucie," he told me, "I ain't cut out to take orders. There's no way I was gonna get a job working for someone else."

As someone who doesn't like being told what to do living in a world where most jobs consist of doing whatever someone tells you to do, Jimmy knew he had a dilemma. So when he was in high school, he'd already started thinking about what he wanted to do when he got out. He had lots of ideas, but the one he ran with was for a restaurant.

Starting a restaurant had a lot of startup costs, though, and Jimmy didn't have six figures of cash lying around or the means to get a big loan, so he had to be creative.

I'm dating myself with this story, but back in the day, most strip mall parking lots had little huts, no bigger than about 10 feet by 10 feet, that contained one of two types of businesses.

The first was a one-hour photo mat. These were places where you could drive up to a window and drop off your camera film (if you don't know what camera film is, check Wikipedia or visit the Smithsonian). Then, the person inside would drop them into the developing machine and hand them to you out the window when you came back after an hour or so.

The other kind of business was a key cutter (if you don't know what a key is, check Wikipedia or visit the Smithsonian). These places didn't take an hour. You could just drive up, hand the person in the hut a key through the window, and in under a minute, they would hand you a duplicate.

Both of these businesses had a similar physical footprint. A small hut, maybe 10x10, with a drive-up window. Inside, there was just enough room for the equipment and a person to stand up.

As film developing and key cutting moved from highly specialized tasks that were performed in parking lot huts to commodity tasks that were taken over by drug and hardware stores, these little buildings went vacant. And since there really weren't a lot of businesses that could work in such a tiny space. Demand totally dried up. Real estate developers figured they were better off selling them for next to nothing than paying to have them torn down, so they came up for sale dirt cheap

That gave Jimmy an idea.

He bought one of the little huts, took out the key-cutting machine, and put in a grill.

Just like that, with hardly any startup costs, he had a drive-through restaurant.

He worked there all day and all night until he could afford to buy another tiny building and set it up. Then he bought another one. And another. When things were really humming with his little drive through restaurants, he built an addition on one and put in a seating section. Next, he found a higher traffic area and built a full-scale restaurant. And another. Pretty soon, he started franchising them.

Over time, some places underperformed for various reasons (the housing in the area went downhill, road construction diverted traffic away, the strip mall closed down and reduced the number of potential customers coming through, or any of the various things that impact businesses). He closed some places down as they underperformed and he opened new ones up as he gained cash flow and found locations.

Large-scale businesses do this stuff all the time, but I never really understood how or why. With Jimmy's business, I had a front-row seat to it all.

And every time I asked him about it, he explained things to me.

It was fascinating.

LESSONS

Jimmy was an interesting guy. He was no dummy, but he didn't have an ivy league pedigree. He didn't even have a crabgrass league pedigree - he stopped his education at high school.

But he taught himself a lot, he solved problems with logic.

Working for Jimmy was different than a lot of other jobs I had. I wasn't working for some faceless multinational conglomerate. I was working for a person.

And this person taught me a lot.

He explained the decisions that had to be made and why.

When decisions came down, they didn't come from corporate headquarters, to be presented to executives, who would explain them to upper management, who in turn emailed them to middle management, so they could forward them to the working masses.

No, not here. When a decision was made, Jimmy made it. He told everyone. Then you knew.

If you had a question, Jimmy answered it.

Everything was simple and direct.

I didn't have to hear about "supply chain logistic back-ups" in some third-world country from the communications department in a memo so vague that I couldn't tell if it was a good thing or a bad thing. But I did have to drive down to Wal-Mart if we ran out of tomatoes.

I didn't have to run three-hour analytic models to see what the impact of a 0.5% oil price increase would have on our shipping costs and profit margins. But when our vendor raised the price of napkins, I was told in no uncertain terms not to give away more than one per person unless they asked.

I didn't realize it at the time, but this was an incredible education in business management. Everything that Fortune 100 companies have to deal with also has to be dealt with by large small businesses. The only difference is that when it happens at a small business, you see the direct impact.

At gigantic multi-billion-dollar enterprises, the problems are at such a huge magnitude, with so many people working on them, that you can lose track of what's actually happening. This can make your tiny sliver of work feel unimportant if you have a leader who doesn't break down your impact.

Jimmy always broke down your impact.

When I went to work at large companies years later, it was a lot easier for me to see how the ripples of my work made an impact because I got to see how business worked up close and personal with Jimmy.

Jimmy taught me a lot about being a leader. He made decisions and explained them. So many leaders at large corporations don't do that. They just accept what is happening, even if they don't understand. They shrug when asked questions. They say things like "because that's what we were told to do" when asked why their team has to do things that don't make sense.

Not Jimmy.

Jimmy handled things personally and he taught me the value of personal relationships in business. I would do anything for that guy. He would have done anything for me. His family did a lot for me when I was growing up.

In one of my more vulnerable moments, he and his wife saw me checking out at the grocery store after a shift. I was 16 and took my tip money (mostly change and crumpled up singles) straight to the store because I was out of food. He didn't need a lot of explanation to know that my younger years weren't always easy (like I said, he was a smart guy, crabgrass league or not).

The next day at work, he let me know that I could eat there for free any time I wanted.

Writing this now, I still remember distinctly how grateful I felt, how much it meant to me that someone cared. This is a management lesson most people never learn. When you care for your people like this, they will do anything.

I don't think I could have ever worked hard enough to repay Jimmy's generosity and kindness, but I certainly tried.

You don't have to try to trick your people into working harder by pretending to be nice to them, though, you can just manage like a decent and reasonable human being and things will probably fall into place pretty easily.

Talk to your people like Jimmy did.

Explain things like Jimmy did.

If they ask you questions and you don't know the

answer, find out for them. This will help you as much as it helps them.

Do these things and treat people respectfully and you'll be amazed at the results. These are the lessons I learned from working for such a super guy.

The most important thing I learned from Jimmy, though, was how far you can get with a strong work ethic.

He didn't have the impressive formal education that corporate recruiters look for, but he was brilliant.

And he flat out worked his ass off.

He conditioned himself to work on less sleep and work without real breaks, even as he raised a large family.

If you're willing to fight like a bulldog for your business and ignore the tiredness that sets in and push forward, you really can accomplish anything.

Now, maybe like two times in the roughly five years I worked for Jimmy, I saw him submit to exhaustion. He just got too worn out and said "Guys, take over, I need to go home."

This let me know he wasn't a robot. It also reminded me that there comes a point when every one of us needs to step back. It doesn't mean we're quitting, it doesn't mean we're weak, it just means we need a break.

Breaks are ok.

This is a microcosm of the work-life balance we deal with in most office jobs, but it needs to be confronted the same way.

We all have to know when to say when.

But we can usually go a lot longer than we think we can.

Working for Jimmy taught me that.

3

RICKY AND THE ROUNDUP PROGRAM

Over three decades of work, I've seen plenty of bizarre things, but very few of them were as bizarre to me as The Roundup Program.

I was working at a fairly large company as a software developer. I wrote all sorts of cool algorithms, I wrote a reporting system, I did web development, I just got to do all kinds of cool code.

Some of that cool code was in a system that handled the back-end processing for our online orders.

When orders came in through our website, a bunch of batch code ran to check inventories, prices, shipping, all kinds of stuff. This was the software that fed my reporting system.

For quite some time, the reporting system painted a grimmer and grimmer picture of company sales health. It made it look like the sales for the entire company were slowly but surely creeping downward.

I double-checked the code. Everything was working great... which meant things were bad.

The company wasn't doing well.

We tried all sorts of sales incentives. We called customers directly to try to pitch some of our promotions. We tried offering goofy contests to get people to order more. We searched for ways to reduce shipping costs and cut margins. We did everything we could, but sales still continued to drop.

Then one day, some developers were pulled into a room where Ricky told us about the next big idea: "Project Roundup."

The idea behind Project Roundup was that when an order came in, we would "round up" the numbers to "help" our customers stay in stock of our highest-margin items.

So if a customer ordered 17 cases of whatever item made us the most money per case that month, we had to alter our software to "round up" the order to 20 cases.

You read that right.

We thought we didn't hear it right and asked Ricky for clarification, but, sadly, we did in fact hear it right.

Being the bold smartass that I am, I asked (for the first of many times) if this was illegal.

I was told (for the first of many times) that it was not illegal. The answer was given so directly and with such a straight face that I had no choice but to not believe it. It was the only question anyone asked, so Ricky dismissed us from the meeting so we could immediately start working on our software updates.

So that became our job. We wrote software that added

random items to our customers' orders. Then we sat back and hoped that they didn't notice or didn't care and paid us for it.

It was the equivalent of walking down the street, handing a taco to some random stranger and then telling them to pay you for it.

You wouldn't believe this, but after the first month's orders, sales were up more than any month in the previous three years.

The sales department high-fived Ricky, they talked about bonuses and all sorts of other nonsense while us developers just... sat there, slack-jawed and feeling a little dirty.

It was surreal. It was hard to believe it was happening.

But it was.

It wasn't long until the sales team started getting calls about orders. People apologized at first, sheepishly stating that they must have pressed the wrong button because they got more product than they meant to order.

Everyone who called got their orders promptly fixed by a cheerful customer service representative. There weren't a lot of calls, though, at least not in comparison to the number of orders that were rounded out.

From a numbers perspective, the additional shipping on the returns paled in comparison to the overall increased sales.

So the following month, "The Roundup Program" was expanded. Any customer that had called in to return their "rounded up" products was flagged in the system so that they wouldn't be given this wonderful bonus again.

Some more calls came in, but fewer than the previous month.

Those customers were flagged to exempt status in The Roundup Program, but we were finding more items to round up and more customers to roll this fantastic feature out to.

Over time, the returns became less and less and a surprisingly low percentage of customers even bothered to return their "bonus" products. The exemptions basically normalized as all the customers who would bother returning surplus items were identified and everyone else kept more and more products each month.

Ricky was thrilled. The Roundup Program became a fixture "promotion" and generated a permanent, ongoing increase in sales.

LESSONS

From a programming perspective, The Roundup Program was a unique challenge. From a sales perspective, it was a brilliant promotion. From a personal standpoint, it was a soul-crushing exercise in ethics-suppression and self-loathing.

As a development team, we were pretty happy with how we handled the technical side of things. It was a fun programming exercise to tackle, but as human beings, it was indescribably awful.

I can't think of anything that I've ever questioned the legality of so repeatedly (not that it's a long list). I can't think of anything that I just felt so awful about doing at work (even though that is a much longer list).

If I was more financially stable at that point in my life, I probably would have quit on the spot. As it was, I needed that paycheck and it was enough for even me to curb my hilarious smartass remarks (a little).

The developers talked about it a lot. We felt terrible. We just sat around saying, "I can't believe this is what we do," while staring blankly at each other but somehow avoiding eye contact. Take away the stress and ludicrousness of the whole situation and still, the hours of lost productivity that were spent on questioning the legality and morality of the whole program were immense.

But it was a net increase in bottom-line profits.

I didn't want to be a part of it, but I had to - I needed that paycheck. I was trying to find another job, but I couldn't get one that fit.

That's what I think of when I try to understand the other side of this story.

Ricky wasn't just going out of his way looking for people to screw over. He needed his job, too.

He was in a desperate situation where sales were falling, the company was facing a dire situation, and he was probably in danger of being fired, too.

He had to do something. So he did.

It was legal (or so I'd been told), though there was a moral issue that had been spun around.

I saw it as a terrible farce of forced sales. Ricky saw it as a safety net to make sure our dear customers were never caught understocked in key items and it was an opportunity for customers to try new products that they wouldn't have normally tried - it may have actually helped them! If they didn't like it, they could always send them back, was the rationalization.

I get that, but I don't believe it.

I don't know if Ricky truly believed it, either, or if he just had to delude himself into believing it.

I believe this was the case of a desperate employee doing desperate things to save his job.

That's relatable, but it begs the question: what else can you do?

That's a hard one to answer.

If it's truly not illegal (as we were all told) and just a question of ethics, the only thing you can really do is quit the job.

But the only way you can do that is to be financially secure enough to walk out the door. The only way I would have been in a position to do that is if I had more money... which I didn't. Ricky probably didn't, either. Most of us don't. If we had enough money, most of us wouldn't be working.

It's a vicious cycle.

What if I could have somehow changed Ricky's mind, convinced him that this idea, which was yielding results, but didn't feel totally ethical, wasn't... totally ethical?

What would he do?

Odds are, he would get defensive. When you tell someone you don't like their idea, they'll try to defend it. It's human nature.

If you really got into a discussion about it, they might even add sarcasm to their defensive stance. A lot of times, conversations like that end with the person who had the original idea (which tends to also always be the person with more authority) kicking the other person out of their office and saying something along the lines of "if you don't like it, find a better idea."

That's exactly what I should have done.

I should have funneled all the energy I spent complaining (which, to be honest, was a lot) into finding new creative solutions that could have helped the company in ways I found more ethical.

Instead, I whined.

When we're inside our heads and we hear someone say something like "if you don't like it, find a better idea," our internal response is usually something along the lines of "what a jerk." Then we convince ourselves that it's their job to think of a better idea, that's why they make so much, that's why they're in that role, blah blah blah.

Nonsense.

All this kind of self-reconciliative talk does is insulate us from hard work.

Sure, it feels like the other person is an unethical villain, doing whatever they can for a quick buck and here we are, paragons of virtue, telling them why they're wrong and they just won't listen.

Once we've convinced ourselves of our moral high ground and intellectual superiority, what do we do?

Give ourselves a pat on the back for being better than them?

Tell our co-workers how right we are while they nod along and agree?

Piss and moan about it to our friends so they can tell us how bad it is where they work?

All that stuff makes us feel better, but it does nothing to solve the problem.

We still have to show up to work the next day and write more code for The Roundup Program.

This is where we need to stop waiting for some superhero to come save us.

We need to be the superhero.

We need to find a better way.

This is what I should have done.

If I would have funneled all my energy into finding a better way to improve the financial health of the company instead of looking for more people to complain to about it, I'm sure I could have found a better way (I mean, I did spend quite a bit of time complaining - I'm a pretty awesome complainer).

Odds are high that the guy who came up with a terrible, unethical, borderline-illegal process to save his job probably wouldn't mind it if someone came to him with a better idea (especially if you found a way to help give him some of the credit).

When someone says something like "if you don't like it, find a better way," we should take it as a challenge instead of an insult.

4

SALLY TELLS A STORY

I've had a lot of jobs in my life and one of the things I've learned is that jobs don't really differentiate themselves. Work is work. Yes, there's the romantic notion of finding work that you love, but when you really get down to it, it's the leaders who make a difference.

I would rather do work that I hate doing under a great manager than to have my dream job under a terrible boss. So, throughout my career, I was always on the lookout for leaders that I wanted to work for.

Sally was someone that I met a number of times working on cross-functional projects. She had a bit of a reputation as a maverick. It didn't take me long to see how she got that reputation.

She got it by dealing with precisely zero bullshit.

She didn't beat around the bush or sugar coat things. She also wasn't nasty or condescending for no reason. She spoke with a direct openness to people at all levels in a way that very few people I've ever worked with did.

I knew she was someone I wanted to work for.

I kept my eye on postings in her area and after a while, she had a position open up. As luck would have it, it was for something I was pretty damn good at, too!

I reached out to talk to her and learn more about the position. In her typical candor, she talked openly about what she was looking for, about the great things the role had to offer, and also all the problems they were facing and all the nonsense they had to put up with.

Some of it was news to me, but I already had a pretty good understanding of what the job was about. The thing was that there really wasn't anything about the *job* that could have scared me away. I wasn't going after the role because of the work (although it was fortunate that it aligned with my strengths and experiences), I was going after the role because it was a leader I wanted to work for.

So I got right to work on getting this job.

I talked to everyone on the team, I talked to their business partners, I talked to their closest allies, and I talked to the people that hated Sally's team the most. I wanted to learn everything I could about what they said they needed on the team and what they actually needed on the team (which, in this case, were closer than most jobs I'd ever seen).

Next, I worked on polishing my story. I wasn't lying, I wasn't even stretching the truth, I was just making sure that when I described my broad experience from my current organization and other companies I'd worked for, that I focused on the things that they needed most. My current boss even told me that she already called Sally to give me a glowing recommendation!

The interviews went great. Every time I was asked a question, I had an answer that showed how my previous experiences could perfectly meet their needs. When we talked about the team, I had answers that showed how well I complemented the existing group.

I even pretended I was a charming person.

I walked out of each interview feeling like I absolutely nailed everything. My last interview was with Sally, and even that one went amazing.

There was no way I couldn't get this.

The last thing Sally said was that she wanted to have an answer by next Wednesday.

I started counting down the days.

Three.

Two.

One.

Wednesday came.

Wednesday went.

No call.

She must have been busy.

Thursday came.

Surely, I'd be getting a call today.

Thursday went.

Friday came.

Today would be the day, she probably just got backed up with some HR paperwork, she was probably working out the transition details with my current boss.

On Friday afternoon, Sally finally called.

"Hey, Bruce, could you come to my office?"

Wow, I thought, brimming with joy and naïveté, she must have wanted to congratulate me in person!

But when I got to her office, her face didn't look ready to congratulate me. She asked me to close the door.

She walked me through the process. She thought I was a shoo-in before the interviews started. She said I did all the right things in the interviews and gave great responses. She said that every single person ranked me as their number one candidate...

But then she called my current boss.

You know the one - the one who assured me that she had given Sally a glowing review.

Sally said that the feedback she got from my current boss was *so bad* that she just couldn't offer me a job, despite how great the interview process went.

We sorted through the details, I told her I appreciated her openness and honesty, then I went home for a long, depressing weekend.

LESSONS

A lot happened here, but my one big takeaway from Sally is this: integrity matters.

Sally had absolutely nothing to gain from telling me what had happened.

But she did it anyway.

Most of the managers I have worked with in my life would have thought this situation was too awkward to act in. They would have settled for the tried and true evasive maneuvers.

I once had a manager reach out to me for a position I

didn't even know about, tell me that they wanted me for the job (which wasn't even going to be posted), and then end up hiring someone else.

That manager reached out to say that they knew they probably owed me an explanation (to which I mumbled "no shit" under my breath, just soft enough so they couldn't hear it) and told me to set up a meeting.

Then they dodged my calls, rescheduled my meetings, avoided me in the hallway, and finally ended up giving me an awkward explanation that basically amounted to insulting me for about 3 minutes before saying they had to leave early and ending the meeting with 57 minutes left.

This type of behavior, somehow, is acceptable in corporate America. That meeting, as pathetic as it was, was still 3 minutes longer than most explanations I've received when I didn't get a job I applied for.

People just accept it.

Not Sally.

Not this time.

Sally went out of her way to give me insights.

She saved me hours of wondering and countless sleepless nights. She saved me from the stunted development that comes when we try to improve ourselves without knowing what we should be trying to improve.

This is how powerful open, direct feedback is.

From that day on, I have never had to wonder if anything she said wasn't the complete and total truth.

I had a positive impression about her and I really felt like she was an open, honest person. Some people had a bad impression about her, like she was a maverick. Not only did her stand-up, superhero behavior solidify my impression of her to the point I never doubted a word she ever said to me again, it also let me know something about the people that didn't see eye-to-eye with her.

I knew what kind of person she was. That meant I knew what kind of people opposed her.

This was incredibly helpful in navigating the politics of a large company, but that's not the real value I got from this.

The real value, as I said, was a lesson in integrity.

In a time in my career where it felt like no one could ever make VP unless they avoided tough conversations and used their morals like chips they had to trade in to move up, Sally showed me that things could be different.

She showed me that you could tell the truth, be open, be honest, and still move up in an organization.

The best part was that she didn't do it for any of these reasons, she just did it because it was the right thing to do.

When she did that, she gave me something way more valuable that a lesson or even trust.

She gave me hope.

5

HARVEY SPINS A WEB

The story of Harvey is the most puzzling situation I've ever found myself in personally or professionally. I struggle to find the takeaways. I actually don't even like sharing this story because it seems so unbelievable that I think people will actually have a lower opinion of me because they will think I'm lying.

I'm not.

Feel free to skip this chapter if you think you might lose your ability to trust me if things get hairy.

Still here?

Ok, I warned you.

I was working on a team and doing what I would call a bang-up job. I was getting good reviews and everyone on the team looked at me as the go-to guy for pretty much everything we did. More than that, people didn't just think I was a knowledgeable jerk, they actually liked me!

See, I told you this one could get hard to believe.

The people I worked with even thought I would do a good job as manager of the team.

That came in really handy when the manager of the team left to take on a new role.

Here I was, the most knowledgeable person on the team, understood everything we did inside out (heck, I designed most of it), and every single person on the team went to our VP to say that I was the person they thought should take over the team.

Of course my strut had a little extra swank in it.

How could I not get this?

And what was taking so long...?

I started calendar stalking my VP. There were like five meetings on there with Harvey, a newer manager in another part of our division. That seemed odd.

Harvey had just started a few months ago. My only interaction with him was at a function-wide team building event when he took credit for my idea.

He couldn't possibly get the job.

Right?

Wrong.

He got the job.

I was devastated. I was confused. But I was determined to make this work. I was the go-to person on this team, I knew everything we did inside out, and people actually liked me.

There was no way my new boss wouldn't like me.

Right?

You might not believe this, but I was actually wrong twice in the same story.

Very wrong.

Harvey pulled me aside to a private room shortly after officially taking the role.

He said that he knew I wanted the job. Of course I did, I told him, but he got it and I was prepared to respect that (even if I almost projectile vomited every time I saw my VP... I didn't tell him that part, though).

I thought he was being nice, working on building a relationship, but he took the conversation on an unexpected turn right away. He told me that it's natural for people who don't get a promotion in situations like this to immediately leave the team and look for a new job.

"Of course it is," I said, "but honestly, I really like the work we do and I love the team, so I'm not looking to just jump ship."

I even sounded sincere. Because I was (mostly).

Sure, I was a little jaded, but I really did like the work we did. I found it interesting and fulfilling. And I really liked everyone on the team. Even though I was upset about not getting the role, I still wanted to try to make this work.

Which is why the next part of the conversation was jarring.

Even though I'd just reassured him that I wasn't looking to leave, he responded by telling me that if I did try to leave, the hiring manager would no doubt reach out to him for a referral.

If they did, he told me he would have "no choice" but to tell them that he was new to being my manager, but his first impressions were very poor.

I asked him what he meant, and he referred to the only interaction we'd ever had: the function-wide event when he stole my idea. Apparently, from his perspective, he felt like I was not a "team player."

I knew right there that Harvey was a power player.

The coming months were brutal for me.

I felt like Harvey was going out of his way to keep me down, like he found every excuse to give me negative feedback and if he couldn't find an excuse, he would make one up.

I know how this sounds.

If someone I didn't know told me this story, I would think they were just being a whiney little bitch.

Everyone else on the team felt the same way I did, though (remember, they liked me).

Months passed in this miserable state and I had no way to get off the team without Harvey railroading me.

In those months, the VP that hired Harvey moved. We had a new VP, she seemed nice and acted approachable, but I wasn't going to go complain to her about my boss (her direct report) when I barely knew her. I didn't want to seem like the whiney little bitch that I felt like.

So I kept my head down, doing what I thought was really good work and being told that, while it had some positive qualities, there was a lot wrong with it.

I didn't understand it; my teammates didn't understand it.

I showed up every morning trying to numb myself long enough to get through the day and go home to my beautiful wife and my refreshing Miller Lite.

Inevitably the day came when we had to do those "career development" conversations that every manager has to go through the motions of doing. You know how it is. HR sends a note to everyone saying "it's time to pretend like you care about your employees' futures for one time each year."

Harvey and I had our meeting. Mercifully, it was a phone call because he was out of the office.

He asked me if I had been looking at any other positions. I told him that I hadn't really been looking. He prodded me and let me know that it was important to always keep an eye out.

If it had been a video call instead of a phone call, he would have seen my face twist up like someone had just told me... you know what? I can't even think of a metaphor for how ludicrous it was for him to say that to me.

I stifled a sarcastic laugh and told him I had heard about a role that I thought I would be good for over on another team.

He asked me if I was going to apply.

After taking a few deep breaths to work the incredulous sarcasm from my voice, I replied with a simple "no."

Then he had the gall to ask me why.

I couldn't very well say "because the first thing you ever said to me was that you'd railroad me if I ever tried to leave the team," so I mumbled some other excuses. We were in the middle of a big effort. My ravishing wife was having yet another awesome baby soon. The office space at the new job was too far from the cafeteria for my liking.

He told me those were bad excuses. After a little more back and forth, he actually told me I should apply.

It was at that point in the phone call where I

wondered if Harvey was working from home that day so he could smoke crack between meetings.

I got him to repeat himself and he said I should apply for that job.

So I did.

I went through the interviews and things went well. Harvey even told me that the hiring manager called and he put in a good word. "I went to bat for you," he said.

I couldn't believe it.

I really thought I was going to get this job. Everything was going so well.

Until the hiring manager called me into her office to tell me that Harvey had given me such bad feedback that they couldn't hire me.

He didn't go to bat for me, he *took* a bat *to* me!

By now, you should have gathered that the hiring manager Harvey talked to was Sally from the last chapter. Hopefully you're reading this book in order (if not, you should go back and read Sally's chapter).

So now I was just plain lost. Despite all the great inspiration I had from Sally showing me how paragons of virtue could actually get ahead in corporate America, I was currently working for a boss who not only railroaded me from getting anywhere, but *lied to my face about it!*

I took a little time to think through how to approach this.

I first went directly to Harvey, but treaded very carefully. He acted very dismayed that I didn't get the job. He made it a point to say that Sally had called him and he "went to bat for me" (a phrase I was really starting to hate) and said all kinds of good things because he *really* wanted me to get that job.

I can't express how shocked I was.

I managed to just nod and mumbled something to end the conversation.

Now I really didn't know what to do. I could have confronted Harvey directly, but I harbored no delusions that that would go any way but terrible. Going to HR at this company in these situations has never yielded anyone positive results. Her boss (my VP) was still newer in the role and I didn't have much of a relationship with her.

None of the options seemed good, but the last one felt like the best place to start, I just had to handle it with tact and try really hard to not come across like a whiny little bitch.

I called up my new VP and let her know that I didn't get the job (though I didn't know her very well, she did know I had applied and asked her to let me know how it went). She asked me why and I answered her question with a question: "Did you talk to Harvey about any of this?" My VP said she had talked to Harvey and that he told her that he'd put in a good word for me. He even told her that he'd "gone to bat" for me (I so came to loathe that phrase that I swore to never use it again in my life, not even when I coached little league and sent someone in to pinch hit).

I said Harvey had told me the same thing.

Then I told her what Sally had said.

The next day, my VP called me and Harvey into her office to clear things up.

The meeting started with my VP asking me what had happened.

I didn't get halfway through my first sentence when Harvey cut me off. He started berating me, saying that I lie, saying that I do bad work, saying that I don't listen - none of which was true (ok, maybe the last one was a little true). He screamed in a red-faced rant, *literally* slamming on the table and pointing at me.

I really had to work hard to keep from grinning as my new VP watched in jaw-gaping disbelief. The cube farm looked like meerkat manor as everyone peeked over the cloth walls into the glass office.

I had never felt so vindicated in my life.

The conversation went completely off the rails, Harvey incriminated himself on all kinds of lies he'd told both me and the VP, everything came to light, and things got even more unbelievable from there. I'll spare you the details and just say it was the most bizarre situation I have ever found myself in in my life (and it has a lot of competition).

LESSONS

I'm human.

I like to feel like I'm right.

This situation made me feel like I was right.

But I can't just dismiss everything that happened and pretend that being right means there's no lessons to be learned.

And I have plenty of lessons to learn.

I need to look back at what happened and see what I could have done differently.

If I go back to the end of the story where things were happily resolved, I see one big lesson.

Transparency is the enemy of bullshit.

When I was in the room with Harvey and his boss, there was no room for lies, no room for half-truths, there wasn't even room for three-quarters truths.

Everything was out in the open.

If, at the beginning of this story, when I was disappointed at not getting the job, I would have brought the two of them together right off the bat and said "Hey, I'm a little disappointed, but I'm committed to making this work and I just wanted to get it all out in the open," things may have gone differently.

Instead, I let nervous hesitation keep me from acting. I barely knew my new boss (except for one mostly bad interaction) and I knew the new VP even less.

Talk about tough.

It's hard to walk into a room with those two characters and be open and vulnerable.

But if I sucked it up and did something tough, I could have avoided the far tougher situations that came. Not only could it have saved me a ton of future grief, it could have established me as an open, honest, transparent, and *trustable* communicator right off the bat.

I could have shown the same bold honesty that I would later learn from Sally.

It would have also established a better relationship with my new VP so I would have a little more credibility in any conversation going forward.

At the end of the story, it wasn't until we talked more that things cleared up. Had I done this sooner, things may have been clearer much earlier. At the very least, I probably would have had better relationships with both of them.

I learned some good lessons here.

I also have to think about what I learned from Harvey's perspective.

It would be too easy (and really tempting) to just say "I learned he's a big dickhead."

That wouldn't help anything.

It's hard for me to try to understand Harvey's perspective since we never spoke a word to each other again after the blowup meeting, but I need to try if I want to learn anything from this ordeal.

If I don't, I end up just walking around thinking he's some kind of cardboard cutout villain.

That's never the case.

People don't do things for no reason. If we want to learn anything from situations like this, we need to understand why they did the things they did, *especially* when we don't understand or agree with them.

In this case, since I don't understand what he was thinking, I have to look at everything I know about him to try to find the lessons.

My first experience with him was when he stole credit for an idea he didn't have. Then, he figured out how to get the manager job for my team, despite not having any experience with our work and being very new at our company.

Some things that he shared about himself when he

took the role were that he had a lot of management experience and had gone through a prestigious management development program at one of the largest and most well-known companies in the world.

So he saw himself as a leader. He didn't believe that he needed to be a subject matter expert to lead a team effectively. This isn't necessarily an incorrect position.

Jim Hackett, the CEO of Ford, wasn't a mechanic. Ramon Laguarta, the CEO of PepsiCo, didn't have a master's degree in taste chemistry. Jeff Bezos built Amazon, a company that started off as a book retailer and became known for its amazing logistics department, but Bezos was neither an author nor a truck driver.

It's ok to be a non-expert leader.

Non-expert leaders can be very successful. They focus less on getting into the details of the day-to-day work and they focus more on building relationships to establish credibility and enabling the team to get work done.

Harvey clearly leaned on his strength in relationship building. In his short time at the company, he'd built relationships with a lot of influential people, including my old VP, who he convinced to hire him.

But I think he took a wrong turn at the second part of being a good non-expert leader: enabling the team to get work done.

Instead of reaching out to key team members to establish relationships and enable, empower, and champion them, his first action as manager was to let the most knowledgeable subject matter expert know that he wasn't going to let them go anywhere.

It was like he'd used up all his relationship energy on

upward relationships and just took a shortcut straight to coercion for his downward relationships.

Being a non-expert leader requires a different approach. It doesn't take long for people to figure out if they know more than you do on a topic. The best path to being a non-expert leader requires embracing that.

Harvey could have taken a transparent path and sat down with the entire team when he first got the role and said something like "Hey guys, I'm really excited to be leading this team, but I don't have the knowledge you guys have. I know you've been here a while and have been doing a great job. I'm going to be depending on all of you to teach me about your work and keep that high standard of quality."

This requires humility, self-awareness, and vulnerability.

These traits are often seen as a weakness by leaders who view promotions as power grabs. But for servant leaders, inspiring managers who make it to the highest levels of success, these traits are the building blocks of everything (see The Power of Vulnerability by Brené Brown or any biography on Gandhi to learn more).

Harvey took the path of a power player rather than a servant leader.

That's my initial read on it, but maybe I'm wrong, maybe there's more to it.

The only way we can develop and improve is by looking at the past and finding ways to do better in the future.

In this case, I'm assuming what his motivation was. Maybe his motivation was different than I assumed.

Maybe he thought the company was better off with me on this team. Maybe he wasn't trying to keep me around for personal power reasons, but was actually just looking out for the greater good in his own way.

If that was the case, I still think there's a lot to learn.

The way Harvey went about this made me miserable (side note: any time you make someone miserable, it should be a red flag that you aren't doing it right). If someone is so valuable that you feel the need to keep them in place for the good of the company, you might want to try an approach that doesn't make them miserable.

When I knew I didn't have a chance to move somewhere else in the company, I started looking outside the company. Had I taken a job outside the company, it would have been far worse for the organization than if I had simply moved teams internally.

So how can you find a balance?

There's some part of human nature that wants to manage with a clenched fist instead of an open palm. You catch more bees with honey than vinegar and you keep more employees by being nice instead of by being a total jerkface.

I promise you: being a total jerkface is not the best way to keep people working for you.

It's not even top 5.

There's a lot of positive ways to keep people working for you, starting with just being a decent and reasonable human being to them.

Maybe a raise would make them stay in place. Money isn't the end all be all motivator, but most people go to work every day so they can pay their bills every month and eat every day.

In fact, sometimes people's life circumstances get to the point where they feel like they need to leave a job they are perfectly content at so they can earn more to support their family or lifestyle. Preemptively giving a key employee a raise can take one more reason for them to leave off the list (but I can't stress enough that not being a jerk boss is a great way to take another reason off the list).

When you really want someone to stay in one place, you can just approach them and said "Hey, we think you're doing great work. We think you're an important part of the team and we really want you to stay. I went ahead and got you a raise. It's not a life-changing amount of money, but I hope it lets you know how much we appreciate and value you."

Imagine how far that would go.

That's really 1% management right there. That makes people feel good. That makes people want to stick around instead of feeling like a caged rat, hissing and biting every finger that gets near them.

I know that HR can be stingy with raises, but a spot bonus also has a way of helping someone feel appreciated, too. It's not even the money that matters, it's the thought that someone went out of their way to do something that they didn't have to do just to let you know that they cared.

That's powerful.

If you don't have the ability to get any financial rewards through the company, there are still a lot of things you can do. Take them out for lunch (maybe you can expense it), buy them a gift card (you can even - gasp - use your own money), or even just write them a little note.

A hand-written card that says "Hey, I notice the work you do. It's important and it matters. You're an integral part of our team and everything we do. I just want you to know how much I appreciate it. Thank you." can go a long way in making someone feel appreciated.

I have a stack of these that I've received over the years. I can't bring myself to toss them out because they were that meaningful.

Check out the book The 5 Love Languages of Appreciation in the Workplace by Chapman and White. It talks about how different people appreciate different types of rewards (for example some people prefer words of affirmation over physical gifts).

If Harvey had read that book, I might have had a completely different story to share in this book.

He definitely didn't make me feel good about staying on the team. But maybe that wasn't his intention, either. Maybe he had some developmental feedback areas for me. Maybe he thought there were some things that I needed to work on before I moved on to another area.

It's totally possible that he was looking out for my personal development and just went about it in a less-than-optimal manner. Maybe he thought more time on the team, under his leadership, would serve me and the company well. Maybe he had some real feedback for me on developmental areas and thought they would limit the team and myself.

If that was the case, he would have been better served

by finding the managerial courage to give that feedback in a straightforward manner.

People see things through their own perspective. It's a lot easier for someone who isn't me to see my flaws (no matter how amazing I think I am).

It can be hard to see flaws, however valid, in someone and talk to them about it, however helpful it may be. We fear people's reactions because, well, people usually don't react well to being told they have flaws.

So we avoid telling them.

This is no way to develop people.

Developing people is hard.

Having productive feedback conversations is hard.

It can be useless if we sugar-coat our feedback so much that we don't resonate with someone, but, as this story shows, it can be even more damaging if we take a "tough love" approach.

This entire episode was the worst season of my career. I think about it a lot when I think about what kind of manager I want to be and how I can avoid making people feel bad.

As humans, we have a tendency to shy away from tough conversations. We look for shortcuts in the name of efficiency. But shortcuts don't work in personal development and feedback. The only way to have an impact is to take the time and energy and emotion to do it right.

In all the possible explanations of the behavior in this case, it can be tough to sort through the best course of action. One way to help is to just ask yourself at any tough decision: am I making the person better or the company better by my actions?

6

MEGAN TAKES ACTION

Last chapter, I said you should have been reading this book in order. If you haven't done that yet, you should go back and look at the last two chapters - Megan's story builds off of those.

Megan became my vice president shortly after her predecessor had passed me over for a promotion to give it to someone who was new to the company.

Megan was the one I called after Harvey told me she went to bat for me (man, I really hate that phrase) and Sally told me he gave terrible feedback. It was hard for me to even reach out to Megan. I was very nervous about how she would handle it and it took a lot of emotional channeling to work up the courage to tell her.

But I had to have that difficult conversation. Nothing good ever comes of avoiding a difficult, but necessary, conversation.

Wasting no time, Megan immediately got the three of us in a room to hash through it. Harvey erupted, slamming the table in a contradicting tirade that let everyone else in the room know all the things he'd been lying about.

Through it all, Megan practiced restraint and active listening in a way I didn't think was possible. When the yelling stopped, Megan, far calmer than I could have ever been, looked to both of us and quietly said, "I need some time to think through this," then dismissed us.

I went back to my desk and barely got my butt in my chair when my phone rang. It was Megan. She asked me if I had lunch plans. I said no. She said, "good, let's go right now."

It was hard to make small talk on the way to the cafeteria after that, so we walked quietly, got our food, then sat down. She placed her hands on the table, looked me dead in the eye and said, "I'm sorry."

I was taken aback.

I had no idea what to expect, but I wasn't expecting that.

Megan seemed like a nice person, but as my boss's boss, we didn't have a close relationship, certainly nothing that would make me think she would need to apologize.

No one apologizes at work.

Oh sure, if you almost bump into each other, you step to the side and sheepishly mumble "sorry" but that's about it.

With full sincerity, she said, "I'm sorry. I had no idea it was that bad."

I don't think any sentence in my career ever made me feel so good.

She nodded, and cleared her throat and said, "effective

immediately, you report to me. I don't know what else is going to happen, but I'm not going to make you do that anymore."

I felt like my wife had given birth, Packers had won the Super Bowl, and I had been told I had won a lifetime supply of Miller Lite all at the same time.

In the span of four sentences, she had earned my eternal gratitude and over the coming months, she earned my lifelong loyalty.

Megan was a busy VP, but when she said I was going to report to her, she meant it. She didn't just kinda-sorta take me on, she was involved in everything I did.

I'd had absentee managers before and honestly, I would have loved that at this point after what I had gone through. Instead, Megan became the most engaged leader I'd ever had in my career.

There was no way I could do anything but ramp up my effort when working for her.

She was an incredible manager on top of it all. A great relationship-builder, an amazing servant leader, a top-notch strategist, an exceptional tactician, a phenomenal partner, a tremendous coach - she was the kind of leader that makes you empty a thesaurus trying to describe.

I stayed on her team as long as I could. The day she left was a sad day, but in the time I worked for her, I learned more about being a leader than I did from almost every other manager I ever had combined.

I could write a four-book series on leadership based completely on what I learned from her and still have tales left over to tell at the bar. She was phenomenal, but it all started with one incident.

There was something difficult, and she didn't hesitate to address it. She acted swiftly and decisively, despite what a tough situation it was.

LESSONS

Megan could have handled the Harvey explosion in a number of ways. She could have never gotten involved. This is what a lot of VPs would do. They don't get paid to referee petty squabbles between middle managers and their underlings. "Figure it out" and "Manage your boss" are a couple ways higher-ups dismiss things like this.

She could have been a sympathetic coach. She could have said something like "That must be so hard for you. I understand why you're frustrated. Have you tried talking directly to her?" Managers like this may or may not actually care, but they definitely don't want to get their hands dirty.

This doesn't mean that they don't care, per se. They might just feel like they would be micromanaging if they got involved with something a couple levels beneath them. Or they may just be too busy - it literally isn't in their job description.

They may also want to trust their direct reports to handle things below them. They may view this as a necessary part of being an empowering leader.

All of these reasons are logical and perfectly acceptable, but what I learned from Megan is that at some point, there is a line that has to be drawn. At some point, you have to get involved. An airline pilot can't watch an engine go out mid-flight and say "Welp, that's the mechanic's problem." They have to take action.

Megan took action.

It was a difficult situation and she could have used a number of excuses to avoid getting involved.

Instead of calling up any of the excuses, she dove in and got her hands dirty. She took on a gigantic headache because it was the right move to help me, it was the right move to keep her team on track, and it was the right move for the company to get all this stuff in order.

Be an empowering leader, let your people control things, but also make sure you're paying close enough attention to see when something goes off the rails. At that point, you have to jump in, no matter how painful and messy it is.

7

DON MAKES A TOUGH CALL

I vividly remember the best team I ever worked on. I had an amazingly supportive boss, a team of people who all showed up to work every day ready to kick ass, and everyone was super fun to be around.

It was like working in a stock photo.

Like all good things, it eventually came to an end.

Our company was undergoing some major re-orgs to transform the look of the entire organization.

My team was still showing up every day and kicking ass, but with the re-orgs, everything was up for debate.

My functional head, Don, was super stressed. He was extremely capable and great at his job, but the pressures and demands that were put on him by the executive committee were really getting to him.

We knew things were going bad, but my team felt the best way we could make things easier on him was to keep doing awesome work so that our responsibilities would be one thing that he wouldn't have to worry about on the laundry list of crap that he had to worry about.

So we did.

Things were going great. Our clients were happy, we were hitting all our metrics, and even making progress on a couple new ideas that weren't even on our objectives.

Everything was awesome.

From our perspective.

While we were busy kicking ass at our jobs and staying out of Don's hair, he was worrying about 2,001 different things and we weren't even on his radar.

He brought in some Big 4 consultants to help him with the overwhelming tasks he had. They looked over everything going on in the function, including the work from our team.

If you've ever worked with Big 4 consultants during a season of crisis, you know how it feels. It's like getting a root canal and a lobotomy at the same time, but the doctor is really in a hurry, has a huge hangover, and is out of anesthetic.

They came in and tore through everything we were working on. They asked us why we did every single thing we'd done in the last decade, took into account precisely 0% of everything we told them, and then put together an entirely new operating model, which they wouldn't share with us.

We were upset.

We went to Don.

He was clearly stressed and, as much as he was a good partnering leader, he just didn't have it in him to really listen or change direction.

He basically said that he didn't think we had enough experience to do what needed to be done (which was insulting on an entirely different level since it made us feel like he hadn't been paying attention to anything we'd done for him all those years).

Then he said that if we brought it up again, there would be problems.

Nothing says "Sit down and shut up" quite like alluding to the "problems" that could arise if you don't do what someone says.

In fact, the entirety of the conversation could be summed up as "just shut up and sit at your desks quietly until the consultants need you... and stop raiding my candy dish."

It was incredible (in a bad way). He didn't believe us when we told him that the plans being put in place simply didn't meet the needs of our organization. We had example after example comparing what we'd been doing to what they were implementing and showing a gigantic gap analysis.

But he didn't listen.

We'd been making him look brilliant for years. Person for person, I think our team was out-performing every team in the company (we had to have been at least top 5).

But he didn't listen to us.

It didn't really bother me that these consultants (who between the three of them had less education and experience combined as I did) put together a generic model (two of my friends at companies in different industries had received basically a carbon copy of the plan from their Big 4 consultants) that didn't meet our needs (they had no idea how the looming giant regulatory effort that could end our company worked). No, that didn't really bother me (well, maybe a little), what really bothered me was that Don took the words of these strangers instead of listening to the superstar team who had loyally served him with consistently top-notch results for years.

It was insulting.

It was heartbreaking.

The results didn't matter (the whole thing was a disaster, and the function was dismantled), what mattered was how it made us *feel*.

LESSONS

I'll try really hard to not make this story a lesson in bad consulting.

If I do that, I take the easy route. I absolve myself of all blame and overlook any chance for self-improvement.

And as much as I like easy routes and absolving myself of blame, I don't feel like it's useful.

First, I have to come to terms with the fact that consultants aren't evil villains putting elaborate plans in place just to piss me off and ruin companies.

They're brought in to do a job and they do the best they can. Let's not dwell on the conflict of interest that could arise if they were able to get rich by prolonging problems. Instead, let's assume they came in and did the best job they could to help.

We could talk about how they handled their partnership, but I'd be wasting everyone's time. Big 4 consultants are trained to do things a certain way, even if they don't agree with it. It's like the military. None of them are going to read this book and change their ways, so let's hold them as a constant variable in this equation.

Then let's look to Don.

Don really is a smart leader, he's one of my favorite VPs of all time (which is why this one stung so much).

So what was going through his mind here?

It's clear he was stressed. We can't underestimate the impact that can have on someone.

He may have truly feared for our team and tried to use the consultants as a proverbial shit shield so that if anything went wrong, we wouldn't be to blame.

When the stakes are high for executives, this is a very real fear. If this was the case, he (and the company), would have been better served had he been more understanding when we came to him.

If he would have taken a deep breath and said "Look guys, times are really hard. There's a lot going on at levels that I can't discuss with you. I hope you understand, but I need to have a third party in here to take the lead. I know you're great and I remember problems x, y, and z, and your team did fantastic. But right now, I'm sorry, we have to bring in an outside firm to manage this. Please try to work with them and my door is always open."

That doesn't sound like "sit down and shut up." That sounds like an empathetic leader caught in a tough position. That sounds like the kind of leader that wants his people to know that they're valued even when he can't use their ideas.

That sounds like the kind of leader that I want to follow.

That sounds like the kind of leader that everyone wants to follow.

But maybe that wasn't the case.

Maybe he had a different perspective in his mind. Maybe he had lost faith in the team over time and felt the only way to fix things was to bring some consultants in to clean up the mess.

That's fair. That happens.

But there are better ways to handle it.

First, there's that whole "ounce of prevention for a pound of cure" thing. Don should have been giving actionable feedback for months (if not years) before bringing in a team of consultants to take over.

Maybe Don had been biding his time, giving the team opportunities, and he just wasn't happy with the results and saw no way our team could have righted the ship.

In that case, as an executive leader, he could have handled it better. More directly.

He could have come in and said "Guys, this isn't working. I know you're smart capable people, but I'm just not happy with the way things are going right now. There are big changes at work and I don't think your team is keeping up with them. I'm really sorry, but I'm going to be bringing in some external help. I want you guys to support them and treat them like partners. Let's do everything we can to make this successful."

Boom. Band aid off.

It's not easy to deliver that message, but there are ways

to do it in a positive manner that won't give people a good reason to be upset with him.

It's also possible that Don's hands were tied; that this came from his bosses.

When you find yourself in that situation, saying something that alludes to the underlying cause like, "Hey guys, sometimes there's bigger forces at work and we just have to roll with them," is a great, emphatic way to let people know what may really be going on.

Still, Don wasn't the only person who would have done better here.

There's a recurring character with room for improvement in every one of these stories.

Me.

I was managing my team the best way I possibly could have.

Correction: I was managing my team the best way I *thought* I possibly could have *at the time.*

Through the miracle of hindsight, I've been able to find some things I could have done better in this situation if I were to have to do it all over again (please, Lord, do not make me do that all over again, though).

I had my team just quietly doing our thing, pumping out fantastic work and not telling anyone about it.

This is one of my weaknesses.

I'm not a big self-promoter. I like my work to speak for itself. I value substance over storytelling.

I don't want my employees to tell me how great they are, I want to see great results.

As someone afflicted with the human condition, I have

the unfortunate habit of believing everyone thinks like me.

So I rarely go up to my vice president and say "Hey, check out all the great stuff we're doing! Has anyone told you how great I am today?"

No, I work very hard to do such great work that it can't go unnoticed (side note: I don't care how great your work is, it can go unnoticed).

I've seen too many instances of people talking a big game and telling everyone how great they are, but not backing it up.

I can't stand it.

I don't want to be like that.

So I avoid bragging.

But, like many things in life (tacos come to mind), I take it too far. I go so far as to never even bother telling my functional head anything at all about what I'm doing... ever.

I have this fanciful imagination that can just see him leaving his office to get coffee and being absolutely mobbed by dozens of people pushing and shoving to get close to him, shouting about how thrilled they are with the work me and my team are doing. Some of my more exuberant clients in this fantasy are evening demanding that he promote me!

That's not how things work.

I know that (I've seen him get coffee).

Still, it's hard for me to self-promote because of all the... "ickiness" that I've seen from people who take self-promotion too far and don't back it up.

I need to break that habit.

If you're like me, you need to break that habit, too.

Just because some people self-promote too much and don't do enough to deliver doesn't mean that you can't self-promote a reasonable amount while doing more than enough to deliver.

That would have been a great idea for me in this story.

Don was busy, I knew that. Sure, that meant that we would be serving him well by not bothering him with things that weren't important.

But (and this is what I didn't realize at the time), letting him know we were doing great work was important.

Since he was so busy, it meant that he didn't have a chance to take the initiative to come see what we were doing.

We should have been reassuring him.

It's hard to bother people when they're busy, but this would have been helping him. This would have been putting his mind at ease for one of the countless things he was worrying about.

I could have just said, "Hey, I know you're busy, but I just wanted you to know that we're doing great. Here's the stuff we're working on. X, y, and z are really helping over in the pencil sharpening division and Project Q is solving all our problems with the buggy whip hotline. I hope that gives you one less thing to worry about."

This can feel self-serving, so maybe adding a "Do you have any feedback?" or "Does that align with what else you're working on?" could have made it feel more like a partnership than an advertisement.

Even if I'd helped Don understand all the things that were going on and all the great stuff we were doing, he still may have had reasons to bring in a team of consultants.

How could I have handled that better?

Probably by not acting all butthurt and defensive.

Consultants are a way of life for big corporations.

We have to work within that.

I took the time to get to know some of them personally. I learned about how one came to the country, I learned about cricket from another one, I learned about the fast-paced LA lifestyle from yet another.

I found that just talking to them about their personal lives and getting to know them as people was a lot more effective than bludgeoning them with my all the obviously logical reasons why their approach was wrong again and again and again.

Being a decent and reasonable human being is a great way to make progress in pretty much any business situation. It took me a couple months into this mess to figure that out. Doing this sooner probably would have made the whole process go a lot smoother.

8

LEON LETS LOOSE

The first days at a new company are always awkward.

Maybe you remember a few people from your interviews, but you really don't know anyone. You haven't made any friends. You don't even know where the bathrooms are.

On top of it all, the dozens of people you meet on day 1 all jumble together in a blur of strangers.

I've had a lot of first days and I've met a ton of people that all blurred together on those first days.

Leon was not one of those guys,

Leon stuck out.

From the first meeting, I didn't like the guy. He was loud, he didn't care what other people thought, he shot his mouth off.

I just quietly sat there not liking him.

After the meeting, some other guys at the office grumbled some complaints about him and that was that.

Until the next meeting. More of Leon being loud, more of Leon not caring what other people thought, more of Leon shooting his mouth off.

It became a pattern. I avoided the guy at most turns and was cordial when we had to talk.

After working at this company for about a month, I was invited to play pickup basketball with a lot of guys from the office.

I'm a pretty competitive guy. When it comes to sports, I can be even more competitive than my typical competitive self. Maybe even an unhealthy level of competitive.

I'm gonna yadda-yadda over the details and just say that the basketball that evening ended with everyone struggling to separate me and Leon and then walking us to our cars separately (which was a good thing considering he outweighed me by about 60 pounds of pure muscle) and the police definitely weren't called.

But this story isn't about a gentleman's disagreement on the hardwood, it's about what came after.

The next day, I walked into the office and passed his desk.

"Hey," he said.

"Hey," I said.

The morning went on with quiet, mannerful behavior.

At lunch, we happened to be at the same table in the cafeteria with common friends.

Basketball was one of several topics that *did not* come up in the hour of conversation.

It didn't come up the next day, either. We just went about our jobs, talking to each other like the decent and reasonable human beings that we were.

A few days later, Leon finally pulled me aside.

He apologized for what had happened. I quietly told myself that meant I was right (because I'm human), but also apologized sincerely.

He also added that he really appreciated how I didn't make a big deal out of things. He said it was cool that I just came to work the next day and was already over it.

I said I felt the same way.

We talked more, and I learned that there were a lot of things we felt the same way about. We actually became pretty good friends. We became roommates down the road. I ended up being the best man at his wedding. He was the best man at mine.

I never would have guessed that would happen considering how much I disliked him when we first met. It wasn't until years later that I realized why I didn't like the guy.

Ever hear the saying "opposites attract"?

Well, like I said, Leon was loud, and he didn't care what other people thought, and he shot his mouth off.

In short, he was just like me!

We weren't opposites.

We didn't attract.

What I later came to learn was that Leon and I had a lot in common.

A *lot*.

We had nearly identical childhoods. As a result, we struggled with the same issues. We valued the same things. We were, in many ways, the same man.

Oddly enough, I would have never learned this if we hadn't had a *tiny* disagreement on the basketball court.

That was the catalyst that forced us into a deeper conversation. Without it, I would have missed out on a best friend.

LESSONS

The first lesson that I take away from this story is to not judge people by their first impressions.

When I first met Leon, he was extremely frustrated at some strategic decisions that had been weighing on his team and his work for months before I joined the company.

He was frustrated and it came out in how he acted in meetings (not unlike the way I act when I'm frustrated in meetings - I told you we're pretty similar).

Everyone that we know and respect has a low point. If you've known someone for a long time and see them at their low point, you know that's an outlier. But my first impression of Leon came at a low point. I didn't have the context and history to know that he was in outlier mode, I just figured that's the way he was.

It took me years to fully understand this and absorb this lesson, but I have worked very hard since then to limit how much stock I put into my first impression of people.

Our relationships with people are the sum of hundreds or thousands of interactions. No matter how many interactions we have with someone, one of them is the worst. If we start a relationship off on the worst interaction, it can disproportionately influence how we feel about that person.

Now, when I meet someone for the first time in a business setting, I usually set up a short meeting with them to immediately to get to know them better.

If I'm going to be working with someone, I don't want my impression of them to be disproportionately influenced by what might be their worst moment.

At the same time, I have to realize that my first impression of people isn't just impacted by how they're feeling or acting in the moment, but also how *I'm* feeling or acting in the moment.

If some clown from a Big 4 consulting firm is acting like a condescending prick and I walk out of the meeting and get introduced to a new director, not only could my current mood drive how that director sees me, but my current state of mind could unfairly and disproportionately influence how *I* feel about *them*.

In cases like this, I also need to make sure I schedule that getting-to-know you meeting for a time when I've been able to cool down.

The other big lessons I've learned from this was that grudges aren't worth holding. Let the little things go... and realize that most things are little things.

To this day, we both claim the moral high ground from that night of pickup basketball, but we also know it doesn't matter. We laugh about it instead of holding a grudge about it.

What good would it have done if, when he came up to apologize, I would have said "yeah, you better apologize, because you were wrong" or "apology not accepted, you were out of line and I don't want to be friends with someone who acts like that"?

It wouldn't have done any good.

It would have cost me a friend without ever knowing it - I have no idea who my best man would have been!

It also wouldn't have done me any good to accept his apology, offer my own, and then still silently hold that grudge, mumbling to myself about how out of line he was whenever I saw him.

In the grand scheme of things, what happened that night doesn't really impact anything. It doesn't matter.

Most things don't matter.

Here's a test: what did you do today?

You probably remember general big items like "gave a presentation" or "read an awesome book about corporate superheroes" or "gave that homeless guy directions to Chik-fil-A" but you don't remember the details.

How many glasses of water did you drink today?

Come on, that's the most important basic need for survival after breathing. How many breaths did you take? For crying out loud, that's the most important thing you have to do to stay alive - that *really* matters and you don't even remember doing it!

If you don't remember most of the things you did today, how important could they have been?

Here's a rule of thumb I use: when something happens, will it matter in two weeks?

In most cases, the answer is no. You're gonna live thousands of weeks, so if something won't matter after a couple of them, it's really not that important.

Sure, it's easy to get riled up at every injustice. We can

point to things that people do around the workplace that make it hard on us and you can go on any social media platform you like (is Friendster still a thing?) and you will find all sorts of people just looking for reasons to be outraged.

And most of it doesn't matter.

Don't sweat the small stuff.

Oh, and it's probably not a good idea to push things to the limit when you're playing basketball with co-workers.

But that's hard to do when you're loud, don't care what other people think, and shoot your mouth off.

9

DIANA TAKES FLIGHT

At every job I've ever had, there's been some good friends that stick out.

At one of those jobs, I was lucky enough to work on a team with Diana.

She was a great teammate. She knew her stuff, she worked hard, and she produced great work.

It was a sad day when she left our team and even sadder when she got caught in the sad complexities of an ugly re-org.

Work became a miserable routine for her. She loathed coming into the office. Over time, she developed health issues and began feeling sick.

Like most people do, she went to the doctor when things got worse.

A battery of tests came to the conclusion that her very real and very debilitating symptoms were stress-induced.

That's right, she was *literally* sick of work!

She kept trying to improve her work situation. She

tried to get along better with her boss, she tried to get along better with her business partners, she looked for any way to make things better at work.

Things didn't get better.

She still kept coming to the office and fighting the good fight. With admirable determination, she did everything she could to try to improve the situation.

One morning, after dragging herself through her morning routine and getting in the car to get to work, a vehicle ran a stop sign into the intersection she was crossing!

The southbound SUV saw her at the last second and screeched to a stop, the chrome grill close enough for her to touch through her open window, burnt tires pushing a gagging stench into her car.

She'd narrowly avoided a very serious, potentially deadly accident.

The first thought through her head wasn't about her personal safety. It wasn't about her husband or children, either.

The first thought through her head was, "Oh... now I still have to go to work."

That was her sign.

When she realized that no matter how hard she tried, deep down inside, she would rather end up in the hospital than face another day at work, she knew it was time.

So she quit.

She could have stuck it out to see if things got better. She could have hung around to see if another job might have opened up in another part of the organization. Given the current state of the company, she could have even asked for a severance package with a wave of layoffs rumored to be just a few months away.

But she didn't.

It wasn't worth it.

Her physical health was deteriorating. Her mental well-being was shot.

It was her time to leave and she wasn't going to drag it out.

It was one of the single most courageous career decisions I have ever witnessed.

As sad as I was to see her go, I was happy that she was getting out.

I was happy that she had the courage to leave with no plan. She didn't have another job lined up; she didn't have a roadmap of what came next. She just knew this wasn't it and was brave enough to leave and figure it out.

She came back by the office to see some of us for lunch a few times after she left. She said her health was getting better, her symptoms were receding, but as soon as she got within a few blocks of the office, she felt her stomach revolt.

She was mentally aware of what was going on, she knew she didn't have to go to work to face the situations that caused the problems in the first place, but her physiological responses couldn't be stopped

It took the better part of a year before she could come back near the office without her body's stress triggering the symptoms again, making it clear that leaving was the right choice.

What she's doing now, isn't important - she pays her

bills every month and eats every day - but her health has improved.

She's happier.

She made a very difficult decision for a long-term benefit.

LESSONS

Diana had a job that paid well and gave her great benefits, she had friends at work and a good reputation... but other factors literally made her sick. She tried pretty much everything she could, then walked away.

I'm way too stubborn to consider just leaving a job like that (I think it has to do with how unhealthily competitive I am). I want to believe that I can always fix anything, that I'm smart and determined enough to make anything work.

Diana's story helps remind me that it's not always within my control. She's every bit as proficient and capable as I am. She's the kind of person I would expect to be able to fix everything in a situation like this.

But she's not Superwoman.

No one is.

Sometimes we need to be ok with quitting.

We need to understand the power of walking away.

It doesn't always have to be on as big of a scale as quitting a job. It can be changing jobs, taking on a new responsibility, or trying a new fabric softener. Whatever is bothering you, stop.

Life's too short.

You can't fix everything.

Even if you could, it's not always worth it.

We can overthink things and make ourselves sick. All the stories I've shared are about diving deep into things that happened to look for the lessons.

Sometimes the lessons are obvious. Painfully obvious. Sickness-inducingly obvious.

Diana needed a dramatic wake-up call to realize the obvious move in front of her.

There's a lot of reasons we initially reject the obvious answer.

In this case, one of the big hurdles is that quitting never feels good. No matter how bad things are, we always think we can make it better. We're great, we can do anything. Mama said I could do anything if I put my mind to it and Misses Johnson told me the same thing in kindergarten. I was destined for greatness from an early age, I shouldn't quit anything.

We read books like this (which I hope you've found helpful) for self-improvement and growth in hopes that we can become great enough to solve every problem that comes our way.

We want to be superheroes.

But we need to realize that we can't always do that.

And it's ok.

Diana is a happy person today. She didn't have a nervous breakdown after leaving her job and she didn't have to move into a van down by the river. She actually lives in the same nice house with a big yard for her kids to play in as she did before.

Her story shows us that we don't need to fear every unknown.

She resisted for a long time. She didn't know if she had the courage to make such a huge change.

But she did.

And everything is ok.

10

WRAP UP

Self-improvement isn't easy.

We can break down stories to find the faults in other people and say "I'll never make that mistake!" Digging past anger and frustration to learn a meaningful lesson takes a lot of reflection and work.

If we like someone, we might call out the great things they do and say "I'm going to try to be like that!" And if we really like that person, we might overlook their faults and give them a pass because we know how amazing they are. We idolize them - we look at them like superheroes and we look at people who tick us off as villains.

In each of these stories, it's easy to have a knee-jerk reaction.

Harvey's a terrible manager.

Don didn't understand how great I was.

Big 4 consultants are just a bunch of dicks.

Sure, I felt this way at the time, but I also realized those were emotional reactions. I wasn't going to learn anything with that mindset, I wasn't going to grow as a person or as a leader.

Those were all smart people who accomplished a lot. There was something I could learn from each of them.

I'm fairly certain they didn't wake up each day looking for ways to screw me over or make my life miserable. They were all doing what they thought was right, I just didn't understand their motivations.

They weren't villains (even if they seemed like it at the time).

The people pissing you off at work probably aren't doing it because they hate you. They probably just think a different course of action than the one you would choose is the best way to proceed.

That's ok.

There's rarely one right answer.

At the end of the day, there's no superheroes and there's no villains.

Everyone is a gray character.

There's no evil mastermind plotting your demise at the office.

There's no Superman who's always right and has all the answers and does everything perfect.

We aren't from planet Krypton, we're human beings. We're inherently flawed. We make our decisions with incomplete information and base our actions on emotionally skewed perspectives.

But whatever the case, we can always learn from it.

The hardest part is learning from ourselves.

There's a lot we can learn from how other people should have behaved differently, but don't forget that the most important lessons come from looking at stories from our past and finding our own faults.

There's no better person to teach you how you can improve than yourself.

Experience is a great teacher, and you have to learn from your own, even if it's hard to sift through the emotions to find lessons from tough situations in the moment.

I hope these stories help you, I hope they give you a little more perspective when you're in the heat of a tough situation.

Just remember to be patient with people, communicate openly, and take the time to reflect on tough situations and find the lessons.

It's the best chance we have to be super.

BOOK BRUCE!

Help the leaders at your organization be superheroes!

Bruce Wolf, who's delighted audiences on six continents, speaks to organizations like yours!

He's learned a lifetime of lessons from organizations ranging from Fortune 50 and Private 100 to dot coms and startups. He's worked for global niche leaders and regional chains as well as small businesses and franchisees. He's worked in financial services, marketing, manufacturing, retail, publishing, technology, volunteer, secular, education, and more.

Along the way, no matter the size, location, or industry a company is in, he's seen leaders make the same mistakes over and over again - he's seen enough to become an expert on how to ruin your company.

That's why he started HowToRuinYourCompany.com - his talks help leaders avoid the mistakes everyone else is making!

For inquiries about speaking engagements (including keynotes, panel moderation, emceeing, and more), contact: Bookings@HowToRuinYourCompany.com.

For more information, see http://www. HowToRuinYourCompany.com.

SIGN UP FOR OUR MAILING LIST!

Did you find this book interesting? Do you want to be a superhero?

Want to learn more about other books when they come out, new talks on similar topics, and generally interesting stuff?

Our mailing list might be right for you...

Do you also want to be a part of a mailing list that will *never* (*ever*) sell your email or spam you every other day with nonsense (trust me, we hate that stuff, too)?

Then, our mailing list *is* right for you!

Sign up at:

HowToRuinYourCompany.com/NewsletterSignup

ABOUT THE AUTHOR

A technologist and strategist, Bruce Wolf has built his career at some of the most recognizable companies in the world.

Working for organizations ranging from Fortune 50 and Private 100 to dot coms and startups, from global niche leaders and regional chains to small businesses and franchisees, in industries including financial services, marketing, manufacturing, retail, publishing, technology, volunteer, secular, education, and more, have taught him a lot about business, leadership, and about people in general.

He learned that no matter the size, location, or industry a company is in, he's seen leaders make the same mistakes over and over again - it's been enough material to become an expert on how to ruin your company.

That's why he started HowToRuinYourCompany.com - his talks help leaders avoid the mistakes everyone else is making!

He shares his lessons through his books as well as through his speaking engagements and unique leadership workshops, which have entertained and educated business leaders on six continents.

He also likes to swap business stories and connect with people. You can drop him a line at: Bruce@HowTo-RuinYourCompany.com.

ALSO BY BRUCE WOLF

THE MANAGE LIKE A BOSS SERIES

HOW TO MANAGE A TEAM LIKE A DECENT AND REASONABLE HUMAN BEING: You Can Become A Great Leader Just By Not Being A D!ck

LEAVE WORK EARLY AND GO TO THE BAR: Surprising Management Secrets To Create Highly Productive Teams In Any Business

LEADERSHIP SUPERHEROES AND CORPORATE VILLAINS: True stories of courage and cowardice in business and the lessons we can learn from them

THANK YOU

Thank you for reading - I truly hope you enjoyed it!

Did you like it?

Don't lie, decent and reasonable human beings wouldn't lie. If you didn't like it, that's ok - you can just skip this page.

But if you really liked it, would you please consider leaving a 5-star review?

Reviews are the lifeblood of any book. Your review can help others find this book, in addition supporting me. You'd be my hero.

Thank you so much,

-Bruce

www.ingramcontent.com/pod-product-compliance
Lightning Source LLC
Chambersburg PA
CBHW060628210326
41520CB00010B/1517